Malone jones

Parenting anger management

Ultimate guide for better parenting

By: malone jones

table of content

Calm Parenting: How to Regain Control When Your Child Annoys

INTRODUCTION

Maintaining your cool, Stress and anger management suggestions for parents Most parents find parenting their children to be both enjoyable and demanding. This is particularly true if there are other challenges to deal with, such as money troubles, housing issues, unemployment, a fear of violence, drug or alcohol issues, or relationship difficulties. Being a parent means experiencing your child's first smile, supporting her in her first steps, remembering childhood pastimes, and deciding to drop everything and enjoy a picnic in the park. It's also about your youngster having a tantrum in the supermarket, wondering when you'll get a minute to yourself, and adolescents who assume you were born in the Middle Ages. Children of all ages require a huge amount of their parents' energy and patience, sometimes more than you feel capable of delivering. You have your conditions to satisfy. It may be tough to establish a balance between the two at times. Maybe you're ready to go shopping when you remember you need to change your baby's diaper again, and your 10-year-old won't stop talking about the school trip you know you can't afford. Of course, you begin to feel bad about not being the perfect parent. Your headaches at the end of the day, and you've had a furious dispute with your husband. Who would function as a parent? Remember A fully stress-free family life is certainly impossible to accomplish, as meaningful relationships, whether with spouses or children, generally require some disagreement and some give and take. However, if you think that there is too much stress in your life, there are things you can take to enhance life for yourself and your children - no matter how bad you are feeling right now. Some parents may unload their frustrations on their children, or even blame them for their issues. Stress may also prompt parents to scold or punish their children in negative ways. It's reassuring to know that all parents suffer at times. There is no one appropriate method to parent. Children from various social, religious, and cultural backgrounds may grow into happy, well-adjusted persons if their basic needs for love, security, and respect are satisfied. Adults whose early experiences with their parents left them upset or concerned may find it tough to handle as well. These tensions may frequently push parents to their breaking point, forcing them to take it out on their children in some fashion. We've collected the finest advice from professionals, as well as some top parenting recommendations, to assist you to uncover the stress and angry areas in your life that may be inhibiting proper parenting and motivate you to find techniques to deal with them. It will also aid you in thinking more carefully about your child's feelings. This pamphlet refers to kids as he or him and she or her in alternate portions to make reading easier. All of the content is relevant to both boys and girls. more of our positive parenting advice. Which sort of parent are you? awe-inspiring father It is crucial to examine this as it determines the sort of relationship you have with your children now and how they will develop as adults. Your childhood The Superwoman and the New Man Many parents are frightened because they feel they must accept responsibility for everything in their children's lives - and do it all extraordinarily well. They frequently find it difficult to realize that some chores may be accomplished very effectively by others and that other things may be left undone. The media doesn't help, too, with its representation of lovely women who manage to mix a high-powered career with raising beautiful children and making exquisite meals - all without a hint of stress, of course. Many more dads are now actively engaged in their children's care. Nonetheless, with his involvement with the home and childcare, as well as his ability to grasp his spouse entirely, New Man is most likely a media fabrication as well. These photographs may drive us to have excessive expectations of ourselves, as well as unrealistic expectations of our wives and children. This invariably leads to confrontations and greater stress. The bulk of us learns about parenting from our parents' examples. This may be useful for many of us, but if we have had terrible experiences, they could interfere with our relationship with our children or perhaps create harm. Some parents may treat their children in a specific way not because they feel it is vital, but because that is how they were treated as children. "I found myself saying something like, 'I'll send you to your room if you don't eat your vegetables.'" I didn't care if he ate his greens or not! " All I was doing was repeating what my mother had said to me. " Others swear to be nothing like their parents and to raise their children in an entirely different way. " My father was always comparing me to my older brother, who was greater in every area." I swore that if I ever had children, I would never do that." Most parents who were abused as children grow up to be compassionate and caring parents, but there is no denying that it may make parenting that much more difficult. It's reassuring to know that all parents suffer at times. What exactly is stress? We are considered to be stressed if an incident or condition causes us to be excessively concerned or apprehensive, or if it interferes with our daily lives. What effects does stress have on us? Stress impacts individuals in many ways. It may make us feel exhausted, unhappy, irritable, furious, or crying. In the worst-case scenario, it might result in panic attacks, sleeplessness, and severe depression. Physical disorders such as headaches and migraines, as well as asthma and eczema, may be caused or exacerbated by stress. Stress, according to some scientists, may contribute to other ailments such as heart disease and certain malignancies by compromising our immune systems. Stress also influences how parents interact with their children, therefore you must understand why this occurs and how your actions affect your kid. Only then can you take action to lessen stress in your life and protect your kid from danger. Your youngster Some children are inherently easygoing, while others are more difficult, which may be difficult for parents. Your accountability A certain amount of responsibility is required to provide us with a feeling of purpose. However, feeling as though you have to deal with too much might be stressful. People in your immediate vicinity, Whatever happens, having a supportive spouse, family, and friends always makes it easier to cope. Your capacity to have an impact on your life It is entirely up to you whether or not you take actions to lessen stress and make life simpler. You can't change everything, but there's usually something you can do and others eager to assist. What is the root cause? A variety of things influence stress: Your personality type Some individuals seem to be innately relaxed and self-assured. Others may be tense and apprehensive much of the time, or they may be lacking in confidence. What is going on with you? There are some events that virtually everyone finds tough - both joyful events, such as a new baby in the family or getting married, and sad ones, such as the end of a relationship or being laid off. However, what causes stress varies from person to person. For some individuals, daily "disasters" like pantyhose that ladder the instant you put them on are the most difficult things in life. Please Wait Understanding stress in our lives It is critical for you and your children that you have control over how you respond when you are stressed. • Be optimistic Instead of being too concerned about your child's negative behavior, focus on and praise their positive behavior. • Laugh Humor can take the sting out of a situation and perhaps help everyone forget about what got them furious in the first place. If you can, try to see the lighter side of things. • Make use of distraction Every youngster will strive to push you to your boundaries. Setting boundaries and adhering to them is beneficial to your kid, but it might cause them to get irritated.

Chapter 1

Anger Insights

We all experience and exhibit wrath at times. Anger is a basic human emotion that expresses a strong feeling of rage, dissatisfaction, or hostility and may range from mild annoyance to violent fury. Many people experience fury as a result of bottled-up frustrations, feeling mistreated in some way, losing or not having control over conditions that are important to them, or seeing injustice, especially when it affects people they know or care about.

Even while anger is normal, there is cause for concern when we are often angry and when our anger is interfering with our career, relationships, or peace of mind. It takes a lot of energy to be angry, and when it happens often, it may interfere with our ability to function normally or be present with people we care about. Excessive anger may also be a symptom of a larger mental health problem, so if attempting to control it isn't working, it's time to see a mental health expert. When there isn't an indicator of anything else, it's critical to focus on avoiding letting the anger take over. While we can't always control when and how we feel angry, we can control how we react to those feelings.

What causes rage?

Anger may be expressed for several causes and in a variety of ways. It's not always easy to find the underlying cause of anger since what our heads tell us is wrong and what we're responding to psychologically may not be the same thing. Here are several examples: A perceived danger to our bodily or emotional health (such as self-esteem or reputation) A potential danger to our resources (such as finances, time, possessions, or people we care about) Anger may be triggered as a secondary emotion to emotions of uncertainty, fear, disappointment, rejection, or humiliation.

• Internal sources, such as recalling a catastrophe or an event from the past

What are the different types of rage?

Anger may be beneficial or detrimental. It is caused by the "fight" component of our "fight, flight, or freeze" reaction. While violent retribution is often the reply, it may also be calling someone out or attempting to change a system or practice to correct the wrong or prevent future wrongs.

Constructive Discontent Simply defined, productive anger arises when we can regulate our emotions and channel our anger into activities that enhance the situation or prevent the events or behaviors that created the anger from reoccurring. Constructive anger may be having a daring talk with someone, or it might be a reaction to a broader problem that demands work to generate systemic change. Constructive fury nearly usually requires stopping, cooling down, thinking, and developing a strategy.

Detrimental anger

Destructive rage is generally impulsive and displayed in visible ways, such as striking out at someone or storming out of a room. This sort of rage has a bad influence on our physical health by rising blood pressure and generating stress chemicals. These terrible sentiments may impair our careers and relationships, as well as cause others to become defensive or aggressive, potentially leading to conflict or violence.

Anger's Influence

Aside from badly damaging relationships and interfering with work or school, the stress hormone connected with anger may also produce unfavorable changes in our brains and impair our immune systems. In other words, being unhappy may lead us to become unhealthy! Furthermore, aggressive rage practices may enhance our possibilities of social isolation and perhaps shave years off our life.

Everyone feels and sees fury differently. Some individuals anger instantaneously, while others may take a long time to wrath. Some individuals are conscious of their rage, while others are ignorant of it. Anger may also be an indication of mental health conditions such as depression. It's a red flag that's usually missed as people don't link anger with grief. There is aid available if you are battling with anger or sadness.

Understanding some of the frequent warning signals that you or someone you love may have an anger management problem is vital. Here are some things to keep an eye out for:

• Difficulties expressing emotions quietly and healthily s

• Ignoring people or refusing to speak to them s

• Yelling, shouting, or being physically abusive and threatening

• Putting yourself down or hurting yourself s

• Increased drug consumption s

• Frequent regrets and emotions of

What precisely is Anger?

Anger is normal, though occasionally unwanted or unreasonable, feeling that everyone feels from time to time.

Rage is characterized by anger specialists as a fundamental, natural feeling that has developed as a technique for living and defending oneself from what is perceived as wrongdoing.

Mild anger may be induced by feeling fatigued, nervous, or frustrated. We are more prone to feel dissatisfied if our fundamental human needs (food, housing, sex, sleep, etc.) are not supplied or are compromised in some manner.

We may become outraged in reaction to displeasure, criticism, or a threat, and this is not always a terrible or improper mood.

We may also feel offended by other people's beliefs, attitudes, and behaviors, and as a consequence, anger may impede our capacity to communicate effectively, making us more inclined to say or do inappropriate or irrational things.

Being unreasonable or illogical may cause people around us to feel afraid, resentful, or angry, which may all be hurdles to successful communication.

Anger may also be a secondary emotion' to emotions of grief, fear, anger, or loneliness.

It is crucial to attempt to understand why you (or someone else) are angry at any particular moment so that the underlying reasons may be addressed and disputes resolved.

Anger, on the other hand, is more than just a state of mind. Anger may trigger physiological changes such as increased heart rate, blood pressure, and levels of chemicals such as adrenaline, preparing us physiologically for a 'fight or flight reaction. Long-term rage may be damaging to health and fitness owing to these bodily repercussions.

How Anger Is Displayed

Anger may be exhibited in several ways; various sorts of anger impact individuals differently and may result in a range of furious acts and symptoms. The most prevalent indicators of fury are both vocal and nonverbal.

It may be evident that someone is upset based on what they say, how they say it, or the tone of their voice. Anger may also be exhibited by body language and other nonverbal cues, such as straining to look physically larger (and so more threatening), glaring, frowning, and fist clenching. Some individuals are particularly skilled at internalizing their anger, making it hard to see any visible indicators. It is, nevertheless, uncommon for a true physical assault to occur without 'warning' indications being displayed beforehand.

What drives individuals to become enraged?

At its most basic intuitive level, rage may be employed to help maintain territory or family members, establish or retain mating rights, safeguard against the loss of food or other goods, or react to other perceived threats.

Other theories could be widely divergent - sometimes logical, sometimes nonsensical. Irrational anger may suggest that you have difficulty controlling your anger or even acknowledging that you are angry - our article on Anger Management contains techniques for understanding and managing your own (or other people's) anger (or that of other people) (or that of other people).

Sadness, death of a family member, friend, or other loved one are all prevalent grounds of fury.

Rudeness, a lack of interpersonal skills, bad service (See also Interpersonal and Customer Service Skills) (See also Interpersonal and Customer Service Skills.)

Tiredness, as fatigued individuals have shorter tempers and are more irritable.

Hunger. Adultery, being mocked, humiliated, or embarrassed, or finding that you or a loved one has a terrible disease are all instances of unfairness.

Sexual dissatisfaction

Money troubles and the stress linked with debt

Some stress, excessive deadlines, and situations beyond our immediate control, such as getting stopped in traffic. (See also: What Is Stress? and How to Avoid Stress.)

Feelings of failure or disappointment

Furious as a consequence of using drugs or alcohol, or after detoxing from such substances.

Having a crime committed against you or a loved one, including theft, assault, and sexual crimes, as well as more minor transgressions such as a sense of being treated unfairly.

Being physically or emotionally unwell, in misery, or suffering from a major condition may produce wrath.

Recognizing and Managing Anger in Yourself and Others

There are typically both physical and emotional symptoms of rage, and by identifying them, you are more likely to be able to manage them.

Physical Symptoms of Anger:

Face rubbing regularly.

Clenched fists or firmly clasping one hand with the other.

Jaw clenching or grinding of the teeth

Breathing issues or shortness of breath

Heart rate has risen.

Sweaty palms, perspiring.

Lips and hands that tremor or quake

Sitting with a swaying motion.

Pacing.

Being rude and losing one's sense of humor I'm speaking loudly.

Increased cravings for smoking, sweets, alcohol, drugs, comfort food, and other substances.

Anger's Potential Emotional Symptoms

A desire to 'escape the situation.'

Irritation.

Feeling downcast or sad.

Feeling guilty or enraged.

Anxiety and nervousness may manifest themselves in a variety of ways.

A feeling or inclination to lash out verbally or aggressively.

Can Anger Cause Illness?

When we are enraged, our bodies release the hormones adrenaline and cortisol, which are also produced when we are stressed.

Our blood pressure, pulse, body temperature, and breathing rate may increase as a result of these hormone releases, sometimes to potentially dangerous amounts. This natural physiological reaction, known as the "fight or flight reflex," is designed to supply us with an instant burst of energy and power. This signifies that the body and mind are preparing for a fight or escape from danger.

Individuals who are regularly enraged, on the other hand, are unable to regulate their anger and may become unwell, just as unresolved stress may make them ill. Our bodies are not designed to handle high levels of adrenaline and cortisol for lengthy periods or regularly.

Some of the health issues that may arise as a result of being angry on a regular or long-term basis include aches and pains, primarily in the back and head.

In severe cases, high blood pressure may cause grave complications such as stroke or cardiac arrest.

How it Works

When you are provoked into feeling angry, your body goes through a stress response similar to when you are terrified. As you can see in our Your Brain exhibit, your pulse quickens, your muscles constrict, and your facial expression and body language change. Unlike fear, which may cause you to flee, anger is accompanied by a desire for confrontation. Your attention is drawn to the threat, and you begin to prepare for a physical fight. Often, your prefrontal cortex—the part of your brain responsible for judgment and self-control—can then put the incident into context and pull you back from the edge. However, the brain's emotional center does appear on occasion.

triumphs, decreasing your capacity to absorb information and make judgments, and you lash out physically or verbally

Not everyone responds to the same situation with the same degree of wrath. Scientists call this inclination to become furious "trait anger." (Think about how some individuals seem to have more road rage than others.) To understand the nature of this variance, researchers from Sungkyunkwan University in South Korea and Duke University studied whole brain imaging data from over a thousand patients. Scientists observed variations in the patterns of connections between brain regions linked with movement, action, and action planning. The research hypothesizes that persons with greater levels of trait anger have tighter connections across these regions, which may explain why they choose to act out on their unhappiness.

What Are Our Options?

Uncontrolled anger may be hazardous to your physical and emotional health, impacting heart health, stress-related conditions, risky behaviors, and relationships with family and friends. It is crucial to detect the signals of rage; the sooner you realize your sentiments, the more time you have to determine how to respond. The American Psychological Association suggests three ways of coping with anger. First, you may articulate your sentiments constructively to define what you need and how to cope with the situation. Second, you may attempt to hide your anger and transfer your concentration to something constructive, but keeping your anger inside and focusing on it may result in more long-term issues. Finally, you may give yourself some time to cool down by moving away from the scenario and controlling your breathing and heart rate. There are several practical tactics for managing your emotions; check out a few to determine what works best for you. We all feel the wrath, but with the correct perspective, it doesn't have to end in dishonor.

Anger Problems? How to Recognize and Treat an Angry Attitude

- Causes

- Symptoms

- Types

- Diagnosis

- Treatment

- Conclusion

Definition of Anger Issues

Anger is a natural, instinctive response to a threat. Some wrath is necessary for our survival.

When you have difficulties regulating your anger, it leads you to say or do things you later regret.

According to a 2010 research, excessive anger is harmful to your physical and emotional well-being. It might also quickly develop into verbal or physical aggressiveness, endangering you and others around you.

Find out more about understanding your triggers and controlling your anger in the sections below.

What creates rage problems?

Anger may be triggered by a variety of factors, including stress, family troubles, and financial concerns.

Anger may be triggered by an underlying disease, such as alcoholism or depression, in certain individuals. Anger is not considered a problem in and of itself, although it is a documented sign of various mental health issues.

The following are some of the probable reasons for rage difficulties.

Depression

Anger may be a sign of depression, which is described as continuous emotions of melancholy and lack of interest lasting at least two weeks.

Anger may be restrained or displayed. The intensity of the wrath and how it's conveyed changes from person to person.

If you have depression, you may suffer additional symptoms. These include:

• irritation

• lack of energy

• emotions of despair

• thoughts of self-harm or suicide

Obsessive-compulsive disorder

Obsessive-compulsive disorder (OCD) is an anxiety condition that's characterized by obsessive thoughts and compulsive activity. A person with OCD has undesirable, uncomfortable thoughts, urges, or visions that drive them to execute something repetitively.

For example, individuals may follow certain routines, such as counting to a number or repeating a word or phrase, because of an erroneous idea that something horrible will happen if they don't.

A 2011 research by trustworthy Sources indicated that fury is a frequent indicator of OCD. It affects roughly half of individuals with OCD.

Anger may come from frustration with your incapacity to resist obsessive thoughts and compulsive acts, or from having someone or something interfere with your capability to carry out a ritual.

Alcohol abuse

Research demonstrates that ingesting alcohol increases aggressiveness. Alcohol is implicated in nearly half of all violent crimes perpetrated in the United States.

Alcohol abuse, commonly known as alcoholism, is the consumption of excessive quantities of alcohol at once or regularly.

Alcohol impairs your ability to think clearly and make sound decisions. It hinders impulse control and may make it more difficult to regulate your emotions. ADHD (attention deficit hyperactivity disorder) (attention deficit hyperactivity disorder)

ADHD (attention deficit hyperactivity disorder) is a neurodevelopmental illness marked by symptoms such as inattention, hyperactivity, and occasionally impulsivity.

Symptoms frequently begin in early infancy and remain throughout a person's life. Some individuals are not diagnosed with ADHD until they reach adulthood, which is sometimes referred to as adult ADHD.

Anger and irritation may occur in persons of all ages with ADHD. Other symptoms include: • anxiousness

• difficulties focusing

• poor time management or planning skills

Oppositional defiant syndrome

Oppositional defiant disorder (ODD) is a behavioral disorder that affects 1 to 16% of school-aged children. ODD is characterized by the following symptoms:

 • anger

• irritability

Children with ODD are easily annoyed by others. They may be defiant and confrontational.

Bipolar illness is a neurological condition that creates rapid mood changes.

These significant mood fluctuations may range from mania to sadness, but not everyone with bipolar illness will suffer from depression. Many persons with bipolar illness feel wrath, irritation, and fury.

During a manic episode, you may:

• feel euphoric

- have racing thoughts

- engage in risky or irresponsible conduct

During a depressed episode, you may feel the following symptoms:

- despair, hopelessness, or tears

- lack of interest in formerly liked activities

- thoughts of death

IED (intermittent explosive disorder) (intermittent explosive disorder)

A person with the intermittent explosive disorder (IED) experiences frequent bursts of aggressive, impulsive, or violent conduct. They may react to circumstances with wrath that is out of proportion to the situation.

Episodes take shorter than 30 minutes and occur without notice. People dealing with the illness may be irritated and angry most of the time.

Typical behaviors include:

- temper outbursts

- arguments

- fighting

- physical violence

- item tossing

Following an event, persons with IEDs may feel guilty or humiliated.

Anger is one of the stages of grief. Grief could arise from the death of a loved one, a divorce or breakup, or the loss of a career. The rage may be targeted toward the individual who died, anyone else engaged in the calamity, or inanimate things.

Other indicators of mourning include:

- shock

- indifference

- guilt

- sadness

- loneliness

- fear

Symptoms of Anger Issues

Anger produces physical and emotional disorders. While these sensations are common on occasion, a person with anger difficulties tends to experience them more frequently and to a higher degree.

Physical indications and symptoms

Anger has a wide-ranging influence on your body, including your heart, brain, and muscles. According to 2011 research, anger induces a spike in testosterone and a drop in cortisol levels.

Physical indications and symptoms of rage include:

• increased blood pressure

• faster heart rate

• tingling sensation

• muscle stiffness

Emotional Rage is related to a broad spectrum of emotions. Before, during, or after an angry outburst, you may see the following emotional signs:

• anger, annoyance, worry, rage, stress, feeling overwhelmed, and guilt

Do I suffer from rage issues?

You may have anger problems if:

• you are frequently angry

• you think your anger is out of control

• your anger is impacting your relationships

• your anger is causing damage to others

• your anger drives you to say or do things you regret

• you are verbally or physically aggressive

Handling Anger Problems

If you think your anger is out of control, or if it is badly impacting your life or relationships, seek counseling from a mental health expert.

A mental health specialist can help you identify whether you have an underlying mental health problem that is causing your anger issues and needs treatment.

Anger management may also comprise one or more of the following strategies:

• relaxation approaches

• behavioral therapy s

• depression, anxiety, or ADHD drugs if you have any of these problems

• anger management courses, which may be taken in person, over the phone, or online s

• at-home anger control activity

• support groups

Takeaway

Anger is a natural emotion, but if it grows out of control or is harming your relationships, you may have anger problems.

A mental health expert may aid you in working through your anger and identifying any underlying mental health disorders that may be contributing to the problem. You may moderate your wrath with anger management and other treatment.

Chapter 2

Anger/hostility

Being hostile means constantly being prepared to fight. Hostile people are generally obstinate, impatient, hotheaded, or have an "attitude." They are regularly engaged in fights or may express a wish to hit something or someone. Hostility separates you from others.

Anger and chronic animosity spike blood pressure and increase your chances of getting another health concern, such as depression, heart attack, or stroke.

Teens who claim to be frequently angry and aggressive are also more likely to be terrified, anxious, depressed, and fatigued. They have greater difficulties with alcohol and drugs, smoking, and food concerns than other youths.

Violent conduct often starts with verbal threats or small episodes, but it may evolve into real violence. Violent conduct is incredibly destructive, both physically and mentally. Physical, verbal, or sexual abuse of an intimate partner (domestic violence), a kid (child abuse), or an older adult (elder abuse) are all forms of aggressive conduct (elder abuse) (elder abuse).

Violence kills and injures more adolescents, teens, and young adults than infectious illnesses, cancer, or birth abnormalities. There is no one cause of teenage violence.

It is vital to obtain treatment if you are angry or hostile, or if you demonstrate violent behavior. You may discover ways to regulate your emotions and behaviors.

Abstract

The previous study supplied the exploratory hypothesis that hostility varies from anger in that it has a bigger potential for doing physical damage, while anger may involve more annoyance and stress than hostility. We studied whether there are expressive variations and distinct emotional reactions between furious and hostile expressions based on these assumptions. To pick faces, we employed participant assessment. Using action unit analysis, we discovered that faces classified as angry or hostile had differences in expressive features and that hostile expressions were rated higher by participants for the intent to commit physical harm. Following that, we explicitly displayed these faces, as well as frightening, sad, and neutral faces, and measured skin conductance, heart rate, and facial-emotional expressions. We discovered that in both cases, faces displaying anger enhanced physiological arousal. When faces were presented by masking, detecting a face was a critical precondition for physiological responses to angry and hostile emotions. During overt presentations, we observed that hostility induced terrified facial-emotional reactions, but anger elicited mirroring responses. According to our findings, hostility is a fear-inducing emotion similar to anger with distinct expressive characteristics.

Anger; differences; expressiveness; hostility; physiology are some keywords. After cooling down after a disagreement with a friend, I wondered how wrath differed from animosity. I've dealt with a wide range of irate people, from mental patients to employers. In this post, I compiled that distinction as well as other intriguing facts that you may find surprising.

So, what is the difference between animosity and rage? The main difference between hostility and anger is that rage is a transient emotional response that is typically triggered by perceived provocation or abuse. While hostility is a persistent attitude that requires little provocation and is typically accompanied by cynicism and bitterness. 1

Everyone is irritated, but not everyone is violent. One is better for you physically than the other, and you do have a voice in both, even if you don't always feel that way.

How Do Anger and Hostility Appear? How to Tell Them Apart So, what precisely is anger? Everyone experiences it at an early age. Infants and toddlers encounter it while battling over "who gets the ball." I know my 5-year-old daughter and my 3-year-old son have continual conflict over what toys to play with.

Teenagers when back on their parent's authority to develop their own identity. Or the time you were rear-ended shortly before work, making you extra late.

Anger is a transient feeling. It is too "expensive" for the body's physiological energy storehouses to remain in it all the time. It's a blend of physiological arousal and emotional arousal. In many respects, furious conduct seems similar to aggressive behavior. But anger has substantial distinctions from hostility.

Anger may also be a secondary emotion. Perhaps you truly feel sad or terrified of something. To battle that dread and loss you use anger to fight at it.

But from what I stated it sounded like anger and hostility had a lot in common. How are they distinct? Here's a chart to show you:

But from what I stated it sounded like anger and hostility had a lot in common. How are they distinct? Here's a chart to show you:

With this explanation we're left with the beneficial truth that hostility is unhealthy for you and anger is a normal element of the human experience.

Where Does Hostility Come From?

Although there is some evidence of hereditary susceptibility (those who have had a family history of depression or controlling tendencies) experts think it mainly takes place in how the kid grows up learning.

In one research at the University of Kansas, more hostile students showed an oppositional disposition toward others that began when they were young.

They came from families where both parents were either severe or forceful, employed regular physical punishment or aggressive control, and conveyed frequently their disapproval of the kid.

Critical parents lead to aggressive children. Those who were middle on the hostile scale regarded their parents as less warm and welcoming - who interfered smore in the wants of the kid and were harsher and less likely to foster independent thinking University students who scored high on the hostility chart were also those who had the lowest self-esteem and felt less accepted by others.

I think of bullies here.

What's the source of hostility? Most of the studies have found it has to do with how one is raised. Especially in research involving twins who were separated at birth and put in different households

Hostility in this scenario evolved out of a victim perspective. Makes sense. When a parent approaches the kid as a hostile or "enemy" and unaccepted person, they then the youngster grows up believing everyone is hostile.

What Hurts More, Expressing Or Suppressing Anger?

Simply because anger is a normal emotion does not mean "just letting it out" is all that beneficial for you.

According to Redford Williams, males who aired their anger only to "get it out" at the age of 25, were more likely to have a higher mortality rate when followed up 25 years later. As Williams says here,

Quote "The basic counsel, 'when furious, let it out,' is unlikely, therefore to be of many benefits. Far more essential is to understand how to analyze your anger and then to regulate it." Anger has to be recognized and addressed. The second destructive use of rage is to shove it down deep within. As Dr.Daldrup stated, "once you start suppressing one feeling you begin repressing them all." Researchers named this the "keyboard effect" like the pedal that softens all the tones.

That pedal will soften all the notes on a piano, just as dulling one feeling would dull them all. Sadly, individuals develop accustomed to that sensation of dullness, but the anger is still there, damaging your relationships, sabotaging creativity, or interfering with your sex life. This typically seems like denial or suppression.

For, I came from a family where rage was largely drama. Anger was employed to shut out or shut up. As a youngster, "anger" or drama as I now understand it, was jumbled together with antagonism.

And for me, the manifestation of rage was always a challenge to the parent.

Young Matt saw rage as banishment. But it doesn't have to be that way.

While dealing with patients in healthcare were several additional detrimental ways I've seen individuals utilize anger:

- Miscommunicating

- Emotional distancing

- Escalating of the conflict

- Endlessly repeating grievances,

- Assuming a hostile temperament

- Acquiring furious habits

- Making a bad situation worse

- Losing respect for people.

Learning that inappropriate manifestations of rage lead to an unhealthy body became the first step toward a healthy lifestyle.

Unhealthy Expressions of Anger Lead to an Unhealthy Body

When anger isn't dealt with early it may lead to "cardiac feelings, headaches, nosebleeds, mottling of the face, dizziness, tears, snarls, or a total inability to vocalize." Stress Repressed rage which is resentment, puts our body on high alert. It's comparable to your body under chronic stress. Muscles tighten up, blood pressure increases, and the digestive process slows down.

It's like hitting the gas and the brake at the same time.

Bad Skin

Even the skin is impacted by rage. According to Psychologist Ted Grossbart, one of the two most "common human agonies that supply the underlying fuel for skin illnesses is anger." Cold

Repressed anger might predispose you to the common cold 10. This largely occurs by reducing S-IgA, the antibody in saliva responsible for viral resistance.

Headaches

Unhealthy displays of rage have also been demonstrated to be a primary source of headaches. Mismanaged anger, anger that is either contained or redirected, has also been demonstrated to be a crucial role in bulimia and anorexia.

If Both Are Bad for You, What Should You Do?

Balancing between the filling and erupting is the primary issue with this feeling. From what I've read about this, the best approach is to explain early where you are emotional.

My wife is Italian, French, Mexican, and Hawaiian. She's taught me a lot about expressing my anger early.

I'm primarily german, which means I'm the stuffer.

One of the breakthroughs in our marriage was when I became honest at the moment with my rage. Then we simply laughed off how foolish I felt. When my German was validated it produced an environment with more energy and more liveliness.

Anger is frequently a warning that something is wrong. Perhaps some threshold has been passed.

Anger is an integrity-producing reaction to the violation of your boundaries.

Gabrielle Roth

Secondly, differentiating it from drama helps us find a space for rage as a healthy expression.

Is There a Healthy Expression of Anger?

From the data I've looked at, we all have the desire to vent rage. It's healthy, that is, if we accept it and assess the "why" so we can handle it.

As Fred Rogers noted, "emotions are mentionable and manageable." Kind man. Makes me want to be his neighbor.

The two most typical ways we show our anger in harmful ways are by misdirecting or stuffing it down.

When we misdirect our anger it comes out as drama.

According to David Richo drama is part of the neurotic ego and fury is part of healthy adult living. It's what we do with it that matters. See what he says in his book How to Be an Adult.

"Bitterness is like cancer. It eats upon the host. But fury is like fire. It burns it all clean."

Maya Angelou

What to know about anger management for parents

• Impacts of anger on children

• Anger causes

• Techniques to regulate anger

• Seeking help

• Summary

It is natural to feel furious, but uncontrolled parental anger may have major negative effects on children, including poor mental, emotional, and physical health.

A parent may exhibit their anger by losing their temper, shouting at their children, or being physically, verbally, or emotionally abusive.

Parents may feel furious for a multitude of reasons. Feeling fatigued, coping with everyday chores and expectations, and catering to the needs of a kid may all make it tougher for adults to be patient.

Coping skills may help individuals regulate their anger and react to stimuli more calmly.

In this article, we look at the impact of parental anger on children and the ways adults may take to moderate their anger.

Chapter 3

Disadvantages of being an angry parent

What consequences might parental wrath have on children?

Parental wrath may have severe implications for children.

If a parent is furious, children may blame themselves. And parental fury may make a kid uneasy, which can influence how their brain grows. Growing up in a rage is a risk factor for acquiring mental illness later in life.

Parental fury may lead to emotional or verbal abuse aimed against a kid. If a parent speaks harmful words to their kid out of fury, the youngster may assume it is their fault and develop feelings of worthlessness.

Children may demonstrate negative conduct, rudeness, or hostility in reaction to troubled parents. Children may also get unwell, withdraw from others, or have difficulties sleeping.

If wrath escalates into physical hostility, it may gravely hurt a kid. Shaking, striking, or tossing an infant may result in major harm, incapacity, or death.

Physically punishing a kid may have a severe influence on them later in life, possibly leading to

• antisocial behavior

• violence

• low self-esteem

• mental health concerns

• unfavorable relationships

Why are parents unhappy with their children?

For several factors, parents may feel fury in the presence of their children.

Parents may endure huge commitments and demands, such as

• caring for family members

- working

- managing home money

- performing housework

- doing errands

This may make them feel frightened or overwhelmed, making it easier for them to lose patience and grow irritated.

Children may refuse to comply or do what a parent requests or they may be rude to a parent or others. A parent may feel irritated as a consequence of these acts. A youngster may take longer to accomplish a job than a parent believes they have time for.

A parent's rage may be caused by a spouse or another adult in the family. Individuals may argue about parenting practices, punishment, or home tasks, for example.

People may also feel unsatisfied or angered if they are exposed to additional limitations, such as job-related stress, insomnia, exhaustion, physical or mental disease, or financial troubles.

These fears may make it more difficult to stay patient and calm when responding to a child's demands.

People may also feel postnatal fury after giving birth, which can be attributed to several variables such as shifting hormones, sleep deprivation, and the stress of parenting.

Everything You Need to Know About Anger and Parents

Anger is a completely normal human emotion.

Rage may be good at times. For example, rage may inspire you with the desire to accomplish a work or to stand up for what you believe in.

Feeling angry and managing your emotions in healthy and useful ways may also help you to set a good example for your children. When you take a few deep breaths or walk away instead of erupting, you demonstrate to your children how to act.

However, fury may be damaging, particularly if it occurs frequently or goes out of control. Losing your temper while angered may escalate the problem and lead to confrontation with others. If you don't allow yourself time to cool down, you might say or do something unproductive or nasty.

Furthermore, children need to feel safe and comfortable to grow and develop, so being around a lot of arguing and shouting is not beneficial for them.

Why do parents feel frustrated at times?

Raising children is a vital and required task. It generally includes balancing several demands such as job, family time, domestic obligations, children's activities, and social activities. It's easy to lose patience and become upset when things don't go as planned when you're in this circumstance.

When you and your spouse disagree on subjects such as parenting, discipline, and domestic tasks, you may feel angry or unhappy. These types of talks may rapidly escalate into a conflict, particularly if you're feeling undercut or unsupported.

You may become outraged by your child's fury or irritation at times. For example, if your kid is unhappy and talks angrily to you or refuses to do what you ask, you may find yourself feeling irritated as well. You might find yourself attacking back in the heat of the moment and afterward regretting it.

Other factors, such as sickness, work stress, financial issues, a lack of sleep, and not making enough time for yourself, may make you more prone to feeling angry.

It may assist you to know that many parents have coped with similar issues with the aid of family, friends, and health experts.

Parents who are aggressive, the method a parent chooses to raise their kid may have long-term effects on the youngster. There are four primary sorts of parenting styles. These are few examples:

- authoritative

- authoritarian

- neglectful

- permissive

Authoritarian parenting focuses on keeping a good atmosphere with their children. This parenting style emphasizes rules and penalties while also taking into consideration their children's thoughts. Parents explain the logic behind their rules so that their children understand the value of obeying them. The parents maintain parental control, but they cultivate a more unified atmosphere with their children.

Children reared by authoritarian parents grow up to be happy individuals. They have received positive reinforcement, such as praise, which has contributed to their accomplishment. Because their parents defined their possibilities, this cohort is good at forming judgments and choosing safe choices.

Neglectful parenting is described by a parent's lack of interest in their children's life. These parents spend minimal time with their children. Their parents impose few limitations, commands, or sanctions. Children should be raised by themselves. These youngsters fare badly in school and are typically disappointed.

Permissive parenting emphasizes letting the kid take the lead. Parents make rules, but there are rarely repercussions. They play more of a friend role with the youngster and only interfere when a key event occurs. These youngsters are more prone to have behavioral issues, poor self-esteem, and depression. This is the polar opposite of authoritarian parenting.

The authoritarian parenting style puts a premium on compliance. These parents believe that children should follow the rules that their parents set for them. Children do not take an active part in problem resolution or decision-making. Parents will say things like, "because I said so," and "my way or the highway."

Aggressive parenting may stem from authoritarian parenting. An angry mother or father may have major effects on the children in the home. Growing up with an angry father could impact a child's aggressive behavior.

The following is an example of authoritarian parenting by hostile parents. Janelle is about to get off the bus and knows she needs to hurry immediately to her room. Her parents resent her presence in the living room. Their tagline is "Kids should be seen, not heard." Janelle has no understanding of why she isn't allowed to watch television in the living room, but she knows she isn't. She walks upstairs and starts finishing her coursework.

Permissive parenting emphasizes letting the kid take the lead.

Breaking the Aggressive Parenting Cycle

There are countless classic instances that a child observes while growing up with an upset parent. The following are some attributes connected with aggressive parents:

• shouting.

• implementing extremely harsh punishments.

• using horror to establish control over their children

• a lack of self-control

• ridiculing people in public.

• extremely controlling

• problems with control

• lies.

- verbally or physically violent.

- clashes with other conditions.

Prompts Regarding the Effects of Aggressive Parents on Children:

Visual Organizer Prompt:

Make a chart, poster, or other visual organizers that compares and contrasts authoritative versus authoritarian parents.

Authoritarian parents, for example, set high expectations for their children and are supportive and forgiving.

Essay Prompt 1: Write an article in around two paragraphs on negligent and permissive parenting styles and how they affect children.

For example, the children of negligent parents frequently go hungry.

Essay Prompt 2: Write a two-paragraph essay outlining the kind of conditions that could contribute to a person becoming an aggressive parent and what kinds of measures parents can do to avoid being angry.

Counseling, for example, may assist people who were raised by abusive parents to avoid becoming hostile parents themselves.

Create an informative booklet about the characteristics and consequences of harsh parenting.

Children with abusive parents, for example, are more likely to develop eating disorders.

Scenario Prompt: s

Create a scenario involving harsh parenting and describe it in a three to four-paragraph essay.

For instance, Anna was raised by aggressive parents. They would strike her if she did not get good grades or do well in sports. Anna struggles with depression and anxiety as an adult.

Taking care of oneself

As parents or carers, we typically prioritize our children, regardless of their age - but you must remember to look after yourself as well. If you've ever been on an airplane, you may remember the flight attendant telling you to put your oxygen mask on first before helping others - and the same is true here. If your kid is acting out, bear in mind that it can be because they perceive you as a safe person with whom they can express their emotions, knowing that you would love them no matter what - and that it isn't always about you.

Use the relatives and friends who live nearby, whether for a catch-up or to have someone babysit the kids so you can take a break.

Here are some tips to help you take care of yourself:

• Pick your battles.

Take a step back and look at the larger picture. Choosing to let minor things go is healthier for your health, and it does not suggest that you are enabling them to 'win.'

• Take a break.

When someone is acting out, it is normal to feel upset. If you notice your rage mounting, tell your youngster you're going to take a break. You may wish to do anything to reset, such as heating the kettle, washing the dishes, or putting out the garbage.

• Plan enjoyable activities.

Spending time with your kid doing something you both appreciate may make you feel better about the relationship and yourself as a parent. It may be a movie night, a pamper party, a game, or a trip to a local park.

Chapter 4

A Parent's Guide to Anger Management

Recognizing symptoms of wrath

Your body offers you early warning signals of wrath. When you notice these warning signals, you may take action to keep your anger in control.

Early indicators of rage include:

- higher heart rate
- churning stomach
- agitation -feeling tight or unpleasant
- increased breathing

- face flushing

- tensing shoulders

- tightening jaw and hands

- sweating

Negative feelings

When you're furious, negative thinking is frequent, and it could worsen your anger.

For example, you may have had a terrible day at work and are feeling overwhelmed. When you pick up your children from school, they begin squabbling in the back seat, which bothers and agitates you. When you return home, your children refuse to take out their lunch boxes and put their bags away, leaving you irritated and annoyed.

Here are some unfavorable ideas you may have in this situation:

- 'No one ever assists me - I have to do everything on my own.'

- 'You kids are so evil.'

- 'I wouldn't be so angry if you acted correctly.'

- 'Why do you want to annoy me?'

If you have thoughts like these, it's a sign that you need to take a moment and do something to calm yourself down before you lose your cool and burst with wrath.

Simple methods for dealing with rage

Step 1: admit your fury

The first step in regulating your anger is to notice the warning indicators. It is crucial to recognize and acknowledge your discomfort, even if only to yourself. 'This is driving me mad,' for example, or 'I can feel myself growing upset here.'

Step 2: Attempt to relax.

When you detect the early indicators of anger, you may take a few actions to begin calming down.

Here are some strategies to help you relax right now, particularly if you can't get away from your child:

• Attempt to calm your breathing. Inhale for two seconds and exhale for four seconds. Repeat this numerous times until your pulse rate has normalized.

• If your youngster is particularly loud, consider closing your ears or wearing noise-canceling headphones for a bit. Take a few deep, calm breaths after that.

Here are some options to try if you have time away from your child:

• Do something relaxing for yourself, such as listening to music, reading a magazine, or simply staring out the window.

• Go for a stroll or run outdoors.

• Take a long, hot shower.

• Tell a buddy how you're feeling.

Before leaving your child, make sure he or she is in a secure location. You may be able to ask someone to keep your kid for a few minutes while you go someplace tranquil.

Your heart rate will slow down and your muscles will relax as you calm down.

Step 3: Consider the scenario If you feel you've calmed down, it's a good idea to think about what just happened. This may help you to learn from the experience and better manage similar circumstances in the future. Consider the following: s • 'How significant is this? 'What was I so angry about?'

• 'How do I want to address this situation?'

• 'Do I have to do anything about this, or can I simply ignore it?'

Anger is a natural and healthy sensation that we all encounter from time to time. However, it may become a more severe issue for youngsters if it feels overwhelming, disrupts their relationships, or is communicated improperly. Coping with a child's angry sentiments or aggressive conduct may be tremendously tough as a parent, and it may have a big influence on family life. Fortunately, there are techniques you may perform to assist address the situation.

As a parent, you must learn to regulate your anger.

Anger is a frequent human emotion. Every parent gets upset from time to time, but if you can't manage your emotions, it may have a bad effect on your kid. Here are some key things to take if your fury is out of control.

What generates rage?

Anger happens when your body responds to whatever it views as a danger. Adrenaline is released, your muscles strain, your heart rate and blood pressure raise, and your cheeks and hands flush. Individuals may feel tremendous rage as a consequence of their birth circumstances, brain chemistry, or medical condition. However, it is generally because something in your history has provoked your rage.

Common causes of anger include losing patience, feeling underappreciated, worrying about difficulties, and contemplating anything awful that has occurred to you in the past. People who were not taught how to vent and manage their emotions as youngsters are more prone than adults to have violent outbursts.

Irritation is especially widespread among parents of little children. It's a period when you're dealing with a lot, such as family, job, home upkeep, and social engagements. You're busy and exhausted, so, naturally, your children misbehave or things don't go as planned.

Other typical causes of anger in parents include sentiments that your spouse isn't helpful, when your kid misbehaves or becomes upset with you, or when you're concerned about things like economics or relationships.

Having a kid may frequently bring back memories and pain from your childhood. If you were molested or traumatized as a youngster, there is aid available from the s. What impact does your fury have on your child?

Everyone gets annoyed; what matters is how you deal with it. When you take a few deep breaths and walk away when you're angry, you're setting a good example for your child. However, if you lose your temper often, it might have serious consequences for your child.

When youngsters witness individuals in their lives grow sad, they frequently blame themselves. It agitates youngsters, which may have an impact on how their developing brains grow. Living in an angry home puts your child at risk for mental disease later in life.

Making derogatory statements to your child may make them feel miserable and worthless. It may lead them to act badly or to feel physically unwell. Children react to angry, worried parents by being unable to concentrate, having difficulty interacting with other children, becoming quiet and terrified, being rude and aggressive, or having sleeping problems.

No matter what your child has done or how outraged you are, you should never physically damage or reprimand them. Physically punishing children puts them at risk for future antisocial conduct, hostility, poor self-esteem, mental health issues, and unhealthy relationships, according to research.

Never, ever shake a baby. Shaking, striking, kicking, or hurling a newborn violently may cause death, disability, or significant harm.

Managing Your Emotions

Anger is often accompanied by additional feelings such as anxiety, melancholy, disappointment, concern, humiliation, frustration, pain, or fear. Recognizing and dealing with these sensations might assist you in controlling your anger.

Storing your fury may lead to an eruption later. However, expressing your anger in a controlled way allows you to release some of the underlying feelings and begin to confront the source of your rage.

Identify your negative ideas, such as "No one ever helps me" or "Why are you so bad?" Calm down and figure out what is genuinely making you unhappy.

Coping strategies

The best way to deal with anger is to recognize the warning signs so you can intervene before it escalates. Signs of anxiety include:

• a rapid pulse or quicker breathing

• tense shoulders

• clenching your jaw or fists

• sweating

• churning stomach

• feeling anxious

If you observe these indicators, take a deep breath and attempt to calm your breathing. Leave the area and find somewhere quiet to unwind. You may also go for a stroll, take a hot shower, or listen to relaxing music.

If your kid does something that gets you furious, count to 10 before replying. Try to pick uplifting sentences rather than negative ones. Inform your youngster that it is their conduct that you despise, not them.

If you lose your anger with your kid, apologize later. This provides a positive example and teaches your youngster that it's alright to be sad from time to time as long as you deal with it correctly.

After you've calmed down, take a moment to reflect on what enraged you and how you handled it. This may help you respond more effectively the next time.

Chapter 5

Effect of anger to health

7 Ways Anger Is Ruining Your Health

Constantly losing your temper might harm more than your relationships.

Commonly annoyed people also report feeling sick more regularly.

Sometimes wrath may be good for you if it's dealt with swiftly and transmitted constructively. Rage may help some folks think more logically. However, unhealthy moments of anger — when you keep it in for extended periods, turn it inside, or explode into wrath — may wreak damage on your body. If you're prone to lose your fury, here are seven crucial reasons to keep cool.

1. An irate outburst puts your heart in enormous danger. Most physically destructive is anger's

influence on your heart health. "In the two hours following a violent outburst, the likelihood of suffering a heart attack doubles," says Chris Aiken, MD, an instructor in clinical psychiatry at the Wake Forest University School of Medicine and director of the Mood Treatment Center in Winston-Salem, North Carolina.

"Repressed anger — whether you express it indirectly or go to extraordinary measures to restrain it, is connected to heart disease," says Dr. Aiken. One research indicated that those with anger proneness as a personality feature were at double the risk of cardiovascular disease than their less angry peers.

To protect your ticker, notice and handle your emotions before you lose control. "Constructive anger — the sort where you speak out directly to the person you are unhappy with and deal with the dissatisfaction in a problem-solving style — is not related with heart disease," and is a fully normal, healthy emotion, adds Aiken.

2. Anger ups your stroke risk. If you're prone to lashing out, beware. One analysis revealed there were three times increased probability of developing a stroke from a blood clot to the brain or bleeding inside the brain within the two hours following an angry outburst. For patients harboring an aneurysm in one of the brain's arteries, there were six times

increased probability of rupturing this aneurysm after an emotional outburst.

Some good news: You can learn to manage such terrible blasts. "To develop towards healthy coping, you need to first identify what your triggers, are and then find out how to adjust your response," recommends Mary Fristad, Ph.D., a professor of psychiatry and psychology at the Ohio State University. Instead of losing your anger, "Do some deep breathing. Use forceful communication techniques. You may even need to modify your surroundings by getting up and going away," adds Dr. Fristad.

3. It weakens your immune system. If you're upset all the time, you simply may find yourself feeling unwell more frequently. In one experiment, Harvard University scientists discovered that in healthy adults, merely remembering an angry contact from their past generated a six-hour drop in levels of the antibody immunoglobulin A, the cells' first line of defense against infection.

If you're continually agitated, preserve your immune system by resorting to a few beneficial coping tactics. "Assertive communication, effective problem solving, using humor, or reorganizing your ideas to move away from that black-and-white, all-or-nothing approach — those are all practical strategies to cope," adds Fristad. "But you've got to start by calming down."

4. Anger difficulties might make your anxiety worse. If you're a worrier, it's crucial to know that concern and rage may go hand-in-hand. In a 2012 study published in the journal Cognitive Behavior Therapy, researchers discovered that anger may worsen symptoms of a generalized anxiety disorder (GAD), a disease described by an excessive and uncontrolled concern that interferes with a person's regular living. Not only were elevated levels of anger observed in persons with GAD, but hostility — combined with internalized, unexpressed anger in particular — related substantially to the severity of GAD symptoms.

5. Anger is also associated with depression. Numerous studies have related depression to aggression and violent outbursts, especially among men. "In depression, passive wrath — where you obsess about it but never take action — is common," says Aiken. His No. 1 piece of advice for someone suffering from depression paired with wrath is to remain moving and avoid thinking too much.

"Any activity which consumes you is a wonderful treatment for fury, such as golf, needlepoint, biking," he says. "These tend to engage our minds totally and push our focus into the present now, and there's just no room left for anger to grow when you've got that going."

6. Hostility may hurt your lungs. Not a smoker? You still may be hurting your lungs if you're a chronically angry, unpleasant person. A group of Harvard University academics evaluated 670 males over For eight years, researchers employed a hostility scale scoring system to measure men's anger levels and observed any changes in lung function. Males with the highest hostility ratings had considerably lower lung capacity, increasing their risk of respiratory diseases. The researchers reasoned that an increase in stress hormones, which are connected with furious sentiments, produces inflammation in the airways.

7. Anger can shorten your life. Is it true that joyful folks have longer lives? "Stress is directly tied to overall health." "If you're anxious and miserable, you'll shorten your life," Fristad says. A 17-year research undertaken by the University of Michigan indicated that spouses who control their wrath had a lower life expectancy than those who express their emotions freely.

If you're not comfortable expressing unpleasant feelings, engage with a therapist or practice on your own to become more expressive. "Learning to express anger responsibly is a beneficial use of wrath," Fristad says. "If someone abuses your rights, you should tell them." Tell them precisely what you're dissatisfied about and what you need," she advises.

The Effects of Anger on Your Health

Although anger may occasionally have beneficial outcomes, it is more often than not destructive to your health.

Everyone loses their cool from time to time. It may be useful at times and damaging to others. Pegasus caregivers in Newhall and elsewhere want you to understand how anger may be destructive to your health.

Anger differs from one to another. What bothers one person may be a mere inconvenience to another. That's because rage is an emotional response to something wrong.

Your sense of being mistreated fluctuates from person to person and from moment to time. The degree of your fury changes dependent on the scenario. Another influence is how long you remain irritated.

Anger generally comes suddenly, before you have time to think about it. Common triggers include:

• An difficulty is produced by someone near to you, such as family or friends.

• Uncontrollable situations, such as someone cutting you off in traffic

• Recalling a past event that was horrific or otherwise life-changing

• Undiagnosed or underlying mental health concerns

Except for the list you build of your triggers, no list is complete.

Other Emotions Can Lead To An Angry Outburst

Some scientists say that rage is a normal emotion. That suggests that another, or fundamental, emotion is the foundation of the wrath. Anger offers a feeling of control over essential emotions, particularly ones that make you feel vulnerable.

Getting upset permits individuals to "hide" sensations like fear or despair. Basic emotions include anxiety, uncertainty, concern, and disappointment. It requires soul-searching to uncover your fundamental sentiments, but the work is rewarded.

Anger Isn't Always Bad

Although fury is frequently perceived as undesirable, it may be useful. It energizes you and inspires you to act. This is particularly vital when you are physically threatened.

Threatening events may prompt the "flight or fight" reflex. Your heart rate, breathing rate, and blood pressure all rise. Your muscles tighten.

You are prepared. You will either run swiftly or stay strong. Your wrath provides you the power to accomplish what is right.

Rage's energy supports people in reaching the objectives they have set for themselves. Younger individuals, in particular, utilize anger to resolve challenges. Unfortunately, it loses potency as you age, and by the age of 80, rage is working against you.

Righteous rage contributes to the rectification of social and moral wrongs. Initiatives to minimize child abuse or achieve equal rights are two examples. People get politically active or participate in legal pursuits as a consequence of their fury at injustice or criminality.

Chronic Anger Is Harmful to Your Health

The same biological feelings that invigorate you may also injure you, particularly if your rage endures. You are ruled by continuous fury. Both your health and your relationships suffer as a consequence.

Chronic anger weakens your immune system, affecting your overall health. Immune dysfunction exposes you to inflammation. Chronic inflammation is one of the causes of diseases like arthritis.

A weaker immune system also makes you exposed to the disease. Wounds heal gradually. You feel fatigued, and you lack a sense of well-being.

Although suppressing your emotions creates issues, so can bursting into wrath. It is vital to address the root of the anger gently. Most solutions depend on excellent communication.

Unresolved chronic anger, whether expressed or repressed, is connected to an increased risk of :

• Coronary disease

• Heart disorders

• Stroke

• Respiratory disease

Repressed rage is typically a source of sadness, especially among males.

Even when severe wrath does not result in life-threatening sickness, it is responsible for a range of less serious disorders. Among them are:

• Anxiety

• Backache

- Chronic hypertension

- Digestive pains

- Eczema

- Headaches

- Insomnia

Anger affects practically every aspect of your body, especially when it is constant.

When You Can't Control Your Reactions, It's Time For Anger Management

- Experiencing like you have to hold back

- Focusing on horrible ideas and experiences

- Consistently experiencing anger and frustration

- Breaking items

- Hitting your head or fists against a wall

- Acting in a risky manner, such as speeding

You may use your rage to influence people. In the worst-case situation, you become verbally or physically aggressive. People begin to avoid you whenever possible.

Anger management does not require that you are never furious. It is learning how to express your emotions safely and beneficially. Tips include:

• Taking time to ponder before saying or doing

• Expressing your thoughts in a non-confrontational manner

• Going for a stroll or indulging in other physical activities

• Identifying viable solutions rather than concentrating on bad features

• Avoiding blaming people for how you feel and instead tell them quietly how you feel

• Forgiving and letting go of the minor things

Anger may become engrained over time. You may not be able to manage it without expert aid.

Pegasus is a Joint Commission Accredited Home Health Care Organization and a renowned Home Care Business. Our caregivers in Newhall and other areas are devoted to boosting people's quality of life. Our services include aiding you or a loved one with physical or emotional concerns, as well as anger management.

What effects does fury have on your body? The physical and emotional costs of wrath are underlined

Nobody loves being furious, however, it's an emotion that we all have to cope with.

While anger is a typical aspect of life at times, it is not always damaging if the body is allowed time to recuperate.

However, fury may wear down the body and mind if a person is repeatedly exposed to a poisoned, overstimulated atmosphere.

Anger may produce high blood pressure, headaches, gastrointestinal difficulties, and a quick heart rate.

Anger management may be done effectively, particularly with the support of a mental health expert.

We all know what it means — and how it feels — to be outraged. However, our experiences with rage may differ: Some individuals keep it in until they can jot it down in a notebook; others don't even bother and instead lash out angrily. This poses the question, "Is there a suitable or incorrect means to communicate anger?"

This is a complicated question. Simply stated, we must properly moderate our anger to prevent bad effects on our bodily or mental health.

What Exactly Is Anger? Is This a Normal, Healthy Reaction?

We'll get into the different ramifications of anger later, but first, we need to understand how anger operates. Psychotherapist John Sovec offered the following facts on rage:

• Although fury appears to be a strong feeling for most people, it is often viewed as a secondary emotion in psychology. This shows that while anger is a fundamental emotion, it is accompanied by underlying triggering feelings such as frustration, abandonment, loneliness, and loss.

• Anger, as a physiologic reaction, releases massive amounts of cortisol and adrenaline into the circulation, which interfere with the body's ability to recover itself in the long run.

• Occasional rage is OK for the body — as long as there is a recovery interval for the body to purge itself of cortisol and adrenaline. Constant and rising fury is detrimental to the body and is usually neglected when a person has gotten accustomed to living in a poisoned and overstimulated atmosphere.

In conclusion, it is good and appropriate to feel irritated from time to time! However, if we don't take the time to control and recover from our anger, we risk suffering from both physiological and emotional effects.

How Does Anger Affect Your Mental Health?

What about the psychological and emotional implications of anger? Sure, none of us wants to writhe in rage or lash out at our loved ones, but we also don't fully comprehend the implications on our brains.

Caleb Backe, a Health and Wellness Expert, agrees and outlines the downward spiral you could slip into: "Everyone realizes that anger is unpleasant, but few realize how much it may impair your mental (and physical) health." It puts you in a foul mood, which may lead to emotions of misery, self-doubt, and loneliness. As you simmer in your fury, you may drive people away, even those who love you the most, worsening your mood."

Anger Management Techniques

Overall, you must learn to regulate your anger so that you do not suffer from these harmful impacts on your mental or physical health.

• Take deep breaths: Breath in via your nose for four seconds, hold for four seconds, and then breathe out through your mouth for four seconds. Repeat a few times until your heart rate returns to normal.

• Concentrate on what you can control: Make a list of what you can and cannot control right now. Then, focus on what you can do to regulate your irate emotions and improve the situation.

• Find an outlet: Put your anger's energy and adrenaline to good use. Clean the home, go for a long jog, or donate items to Goodwill. Convert your wrath into action.

We are all unique; identify the management tactics that work best for you. If you're still having trouble expressing or understanding your anger, go to a mental health professional. Anger management therapy, in particular, may assist you in identifying and controlling your angry tendencies.

Chapter 6
Types, identifying and control of anger

Anger Expressions

You are undoubtedly aware that individuals employ several communication strategies to convey their rage. However, it may come as a surprise to hear that there are five types: Aggressive, Passive, Passive-Aggressive, Assertive, and Projective-Aggressive.

The Aggressive form of fury is defined by a strong desire to impose control over oneself, others, and circumstances. They will not accept no for an answer and will use pain and rage to manipulate people into feeling horrible or backing down. Some prevalent themes are that aggressive individuals deploy sarcasm, humiliation, put-downs, complaints, threats, and abuse to accomplish what they want.

A Passive Anger personality seeks to avoid conflict and confrontation. These individuals struggle to convey their wishes and sentiments and have a tough time saying no without feeling dreadful. A passive rage style strives hard to avoid inflicting harm on others as it makes them feel horrible. They also avoid provoking folks to prevent feeling uncomfortable and afraid.

People with a Passive-Angry anger style are not as openly confrontational towards others as the Aggressive type, but they do not wish to avoid conflict as the Passive style does. Instead, when they are upset, they desire to wreak retribution and may turn to seduction and deception to acquire what they want. They are normally nice to your face and employ hidden means to gain retribution. They may utilize silent treatment, withdraw their love attention, gossip, tattle, or refuse to collaborate. When asked what is wrong, they frequently answer "nothing," even when their body language or conduct plainly shows that something is wrong.

A person who utilizes a Projective-Aggressive anger style may appear to be passive, but they are not. They are frequently highly dissatisfied and are frightened to own and express their wrath. Instead, they aim their fury onto others and urge others to act on their behalf. They may observe that you seem furious, even though you are not.

Finally, persons with an Assertive anger style convey their wants in a straightforward, upfront, and honest manner, rather than waiting for others to read their thoughts. At the same time, they regard the needs and emotions of others. They respect themselves and want others to respect and decency them. They think they are accountable for their own lives and decisions.

How to Manage Anger as a Parent
• The Problem
• Effects on Children
• Parenting Tips
• Group Anger Management
• Kids and Teens
• Resources to Help
• Takeaway

Steam is gushing from your ears. A tomato-red expression. Fists clenched Cartoon portrayals of wrath may appear entertaining, but actual rage is anything but amusing, and parents are guaranteed to feel it on occasion.

Every circumstance is unique. This article, on the other hand, will help you better understand why anger is such a crucial emotion to manage and what you can do if you and your parenting partner are feeling it. Continue reading for practical suggestions and methods for regulating anger and training your children to manage their own heightened emotions.

Why is it so difficult for parents to regulate their anger?

Parents may feel wrath for several reasons, including one or a combination of the following:
• a lack of sleep
• financial stress

• job-related stress
• more duties at home or at work
When stress levels are high, it may be more difficult for parents to contain their fury when even tiny errors occur.
Individuals may feel overwhelming wrath in numerous ways. It may entail loud outbursts and physical displays for some people. Others may be seething or dwelling on incidents that irritated them.
Long-term implications of unrestrained wrath may include terrible health and relationship troubles. Anger out of control may induce high blood pressure and an increased risk of heart disease. It may also lead to strained relationships with family, friends, or colleagues - even with individuals who are vital in a child's life.
What consequences may my ranting and wrath have on my children?
Excessive wrath may have long-term physical and mental implications. It may impact the way Trusted Source functions. The brain of your youngster senses sound and language.
Instead of aiding in the correction of behavior, research on Trusted Sources has revealed that screaming and fury frequently increase Trusted Sources in undesired behaviors. It may also contribute to emotions of despair and concern. Children who experience screaming and wrath may develop a habit of distrust, poor social ties, and harmful lifestyle choices. The stress of going

through it may create changes in their hormones and endocrine systems. It may also result in long-term health difficulties, such as chronic disorders.

reputable source

Methods for parents to deal with fury

If you often experience angry feelings, you should consider when your anger is most typically triggered. This may assist you in developing a long-term plan to reduce angry feelings.

Advice for Parents

If you or your spouse is enraged in ways that are affecting your or your children's lives, you may want to try the following:

Take a step back from the situation (after ensuring that everyone is safe, of course!).

Concentrate on slowing your breathing or counting to 10 gradually.

Participate in a parenting or other support group.

Participate in a sport or other activity.

You may also wish to speak to a therapist about your anger. According to research, over 75% of people who had anger management treatment improved as a consequence.

Is group anger management a valid option? At least one research suggested that group-based anger management sessions for parents could be useful. Mothers who participated in the anger management program reported a shift in their attitude and parenting abilities that persisted long after the program concluded.

Group therapy may help parents overcome isolation and give extra support networks. Some individuals may opt to utilize it in combination with individual treatment to gain the advantages of both forms of therapy.

Resources to help you cope with rage

There are several strategies accessible to you if you are striving to regulate your rage impulses.

• Adults may access a choice of online and in-person anger management programs. (If you want proof of completion, you may want to check into an online program like the one provided by Open Path.) Yale University provides a free online course for instructors.)

• Individual therapy is also accessible locally as well as online through firms such as Better Help. If you are unclear about where to begin, your doctor may be able to suggest you to a therapist they trust.

• If your anger is caused by fears about your spouse, you may want to speak with a local marital and family therapist to work through any difficulties as a pair.

• There are also several books and workbooks for parents that explore anger control approaches.

Takeaway

Wrathful sentiments are prevalent. However, it is critical to control how these feelings are expressed. Excessive rage from parents may have long-term physical and psychological consequences for their children and other family members. They have also not been shown to treat behavioral issues.

There are several ways for controlling anger as a parent, but it is important to get help if you are experiencing difficulties. A therapist may help you to identify triggers and develop a plan.
Do you seem to be continually yelling at your child? Tired of being calm one moment and outraged the next? Why wasn't he able to listen the first time? Or why do they keep fighting and screaming? " Or if she simply ceased flinging all her toys, I wouldn't have to become furious." There are numerous strategies for managing your child's conduct that may assist you, but if you are unable to regulate your behavior, it will be significantly more difficult. Instead of concentrating on your child's misbehavior, analyze what is troubling you.
When I pondered becoming a mother, I felt I had perfected the art of parenting. I expected myself to be the most patient, calm, and loving mother who took everything in stride and replied to her children with love and compassion. If you're anything like me, you've fantasized about what it's like to be a parent: park outings, arts and crafts projects pretend plays, bedtime tales, and so on. Parenting triggers aren't something you considered before becoming a parent, are they? Sure, you knew there would be hurdles and issues, but you always envisioned how you would conquer them softly and kindly.

What you may not have anticipated was losing your cool when the child refuses to eat the meal you've carefully prepared for them, the whining that begins just as you consider resting with a hot cup of coffee and a book to read, or siblings fighting over the TV remote to watch their favorite programs. Every parent has a parenting skeleton in their closet. We're all provoked! We all react, shout, shame, punish, and do other things. We all meet circumstances that simply get to us, and we respond in ways we never meant to.

Those are the most difficult periods in our parenting life when we begin to question ourselves as parents. These responses to triggers challenge our self-perception and create a mismatch between what we believe as parents and how we behave, making parenting more challenging. So here are some tips for spotting parenting triggers and coping with them.

What are the parental stressors?
Parenting Triggers are those that are set off by our child's activities. When they say, do, or feel anything and we have an intuitive negative reaction in response, we shout, lash out, shut down, weep, urge to flee, or we may feel driven to punish or disgrace our children. We may say or do things we wouldn't ordinarily do and then feel bad about it.
A trigger may be anything that happens in the current moment that awakens a memory from the past. We may behave in ways that are discordant

with the present. A trigger usually rekindles an old wound from our childhood, such as not being heard, valued, or taken for granted. When our children are unhappy, we are frequently angered or disappointed by their style of expressing their emotions (whining, tantrums, or weeping) (whining, tantrums, or crying) (whining, tantrums, or crying). It's more often about our difficulties in processing these sentiments than it is about the child's actions.

Triggers push us to react in ways that we, as parents, do not value or believe. When we are provoked, our emotions are often intense, and we feel bewildered, indignant, and out of control. They are almost automatic and sometimes out of proportion, and it is difficult to understand why. They are frequently tied to the experiences we have had during our childhood, upbringing, or education.

Triggers do not have to be anything unpleasant. Our children have also done it. Sometimes our kid is experiencing a beautiful experience that we have never had the opportunity to reproduce in ourselves. Many of us were not "given" independence or freedom. We were never free of unnecessary control. As a result, our children's behavior in this manner may sometimes set us off.

The most important aspect of parenting with a trigger is that you are not reacting to your child's precise ways of behaving, but rather to what that behavior implies to you, which is driven by your earlier experiences.

What exactly is a parenting trigger?
We all have different triggers, but seeing our children experience tremendous emotions is a key one for many of us. It is usually because we were raised in an environment where we were not permitted to openly express our emotions. If we do so, we will be punished, humiliated, ignored, or somehow invalidated. So, when our children experience those sensations, we are sometimes terrified or overwhelmed by them, or we just do not know how to deal with them since no one ever modeled them for us as children. Even youngsters acting "foolish" could transport us back to our inner kid who felt humiliated for being dumb. Emotions may be a potent trigger. But I can guarantee you that with time and guidance, this will become simpler.

Many of us were punished as children for disobedience, so when our children misbehave, we are frequently questioned and challenged. And, depending on what happened to us, it generates a reflexive response. We are frequently angered when our children do things that we would have been scolded, belittled, ridiculed, or bullied for. We feel protective and anxious that our children may go through similar things. We must continually remind ourselves that our job is not to prevent them from being themselves, but rather to show that they are unconditionally loved and welcomed for being themselves. We should not unwittingly duplicate our anxieties by prohibiting them from being themselves. When those around them aren't courteous, we should speak up for them.

Other times, we are triggered because we don't know what to do in that position as we are not parenting as we are wanting to parent, and situations like these may make us feel overwhelmed. I know I have moments like this when my kid is in agony and I don't know what to do to assist her, and I am triggered into feeling useless and powerless.

Triggers are as unique as each of us as parents. Here are some of the most common parenting triggers I've heard and experienced:

• Concerns about food waste
• Concerns about a child not eating enough and health concern
• Concerns about the safety of the youngster
• When children are genuine to themselves.
• Children weeping.
• When children refuse to share.
• The youngster is cruel.
• dishonest Children.
• Children are not following good etiquette.
• When youngsters react.
• Dissatisfied children

- Children who grow "bossy."
- Being impolite.
- Being enraged.
- Children having a tantrum.
- Children are stupid.
- Your youngster is not paying attention to you.
- The youngster does not take you seriously.
- Disturbing Noises
- Mess
- Inadequate privacy.
- Inadequate personal space.
- Feeling unappreciated.
- A sensation of desertion.
- Not feeling heard.
- A feeling of being touched.
- Being offended.
- Feeling weary.
- A sensation of overwhelming.

Many of them are tied to sentiments and emotions, which produce triggers. These triggers may rob you of the chance to be the parent you want to be. We behave reflexively in a protective manner to end our mental agony rather than what we desire for our children.

Some of these items aid us in properly educating our youngsters on how to manage their emotions. Many times, children need to be permitted to undertake things that may provoke certain emotions in us, but in these circumstances, we must parent through these triggers.

What Is the Importance of Recognizing Your Triggers?

Many professionals feel that unresolved trauma may be handed down through generations and plague our offspring for a long time. When you are aware of your triggers, you boost your odds of selecting a good reaction to your child's behaviors. What if your unintended, unreasonable behavior impacts your child in specific situations? Then you may try to tackle these challenges. Before answering, you should typically take a step back and examine the issue. It will only help you identify your triggers, and you will be able to respond more proactively as a consequence.

If you begin to take substantial measures to identify your parenting triggers, you will unearth the foundations of your prior emotional traumas that are influencing your and your child's connection. If you understand your trigger points, you will be able to give a secure and caring environment for your kid.

How to Recognize Your Parenting Triggers
We all have our demons, no question about it. However, once you begin the process of learning about and recognizing your triggers, you will begin to heal emotionally and cognitively. The most

crucial component of discovering your parenting triggers is to pay attention to your emotions and search for patterns in your responses.

The following are the seven indicators of recognizing parental triggers:

When you feel highly irritated, such as screaming, seeing red, or vein pooping, it suggests that you have been provoked.

When you feel sad, unhappy, or wounded as a consequence of anything your kid has said or done to you (which you should not take personally), you have been triggered.

You've been triggered if you feel furious, enraged, or afraid, and you know it once you're quiet.

You become triggered if you feel as though everything is out of control.

If you have encountered this sort of response multiple times prior and it appears similar, you have been triggered.

You've been provoked if you were calm a minute before and now sense uncontrollable rage inside.

You have been triggered if you feel the want to grab, chastise, spank, or physically harm your child.

How do we deal with parental stressors?
1. Ponder: Why am I getting triggered?

If you are reacting aggressively and taking things personally in a situation, it indicates that you are not reacting to the problem in front of you, but rather to something that has happened in the past and has been aroused.

When such feelings arise, begin meditating and pay attention to sensations, visual images, words, or thoughts to evaluate the underlying meaning of these parenting cues. These things will help you understand where you're coming from and how to improve.

2. Begin working on it.

It's time to focus on your earlier scars and emotional baggage that are now influencing your attitude toward your child. Keep note of the conditions that led you to behave aggressively; they could be a future trigger. This will help you to better absorb the events and assimilate them once you are calm.

Factors that may have created worry, fury, tension, or insecurity may be re-examined. Working through previous experiences, letting them go, and moving on is a big step.

3. Change is always for the better.

Now that you've acknowledged and identified your parenting triggers, it's time to concentrate on making changes. First and foremost, begin imagining the possible results of the potentially varied situations. Consider how these various responses make you feel. Be aware of your body language, tone of voice, and the words you use while in the situation.

4. Begin small.

You don't have to go all in to alter yourself. Begin with tiny modifications. Doing it all at once will overwhelm you and make it difficult to manage. You may begin by addressing one concern at a time, such as: what can be done differently the next time the circumstance arises?

Concentrate on the unmet requirements. Our wants being met should not jeopardize our relationship with our children.

5. Concentrate on healing.

To begin healing, you must let go of the shame and guilt caused by the trigger. Blaming yourself for your conduct will not assist you or your child. Rather, practice self-compassion and empathy. You must remember that these are the things that will test you and provide excellent opportunities for learning and progress.

You should try to be as pleasant to yourself as you are to your children. Because you need this generosity to grow as a parent. Empathizing with ourselves does not imply that we should not hold ourselves to high standards or strive for progress, but rather that we recognize that what we are doing is difficult and important. You must focus on your success and what your child deserves.

Sixth, take your time.

Take a moment to calm down and relax if you find yourself in a situation where you feel irritated. We feel parenting is crucial at times, but that is not always the case. You may just be honest and say, "I'm having difficulty; could I please take a minute?"

Taking a step back and giving yourself some breathing space will help you deal with the situation more calmly. Being nice to yourself and allowing yourself some space can help you process the triggers. I realize it may be tough to accept and modify yourself, but trust me when I tell you it will be well worth it.

Accept your shortcomings and apologize to your child.

Another important thing you can do while working on your triggers is, to be honest with your children about them. You don't need to tell them much about your triggers, but telling our children about our difficulties with certain situations and that it's not their fault is beneficial. This provides them with empathy while also informing them when you are dealing with parenting triggers and require some space or time to process them.

Furthermore, having a parental tantrum gives you the best opportunity to teach your child how to form a proper apology. It must be genuine and honest. Accept full responsibility for your actions and assure them that you will work hard to change your ways in the future. You could say, "Hey, I'm sorry for yelling at you like that when you spilled the milk." I was exaggerating, and I'm sorry if I offended you. I'm having trouble dealing with the chaos. Still, it was inappropriate for me to rage in this manner, and in the future, I want to focus on remaining calm and speaking more effectively."

8. Recognize the development of children.

It is critical to understand your child's development at each age to know what is reasonable and appropriate to expect from them. Knowing the facts can help you change your expectations and prepare for trigger-induced behaviors.

9. Seek assistance.

If you are frequently enraged and have difficulty controlling your emotions, consulting with a mental health professional may be your best option. It is not always possible to handle or change situations on your own. Previous relationship triggers, childhood trauma, anxiety, and depression may be too difficult to overcome on your own.

10. Surround yourself with people who will encourage and support you.

It is essential to have like-minded and supportive friends who are also parents during the parenting process. Being surrounded by people who understand and support you throughout this process is extremely beneficial. Some of them may grow into caring figures for us. It is critical that you do not feel isolated on this journey and that you surround yourself with people who appreciate what you are doing and value children in the same way that you do. We are not meant to do this alone, and having a network of people who share our values is extremely helpful.

With practice, you'll be able to assess your triggering situations and intervene before reacting violently.

Even if you are provoked, all is not lost! Allow yourself some breathing room, take a deep breath, and think about your options.

Keep in mind that parenting is all about learning and growing. The more you learn, the better your choices will be the following time!

1. What makes people angry?

There are several common causes of anger, such as losing patience, feeling unappreciated for your efforts, or injustice towards you. Individuals may also get enraged as a result of childhood traumas or abuse, extreme worry, or hopelessness.

2. What does the term "triggered" mean?

Anything that reminds someone of a previous painful event is a trigger. Visual depictions of violence, for example, maybe a trigger point for certain people. Scents, perfumes, music, or even colors may be triggers for certain people, depending on their past experiences.

3. What exactly is the triggering behavior?

When someone reacts angrily to a particular occurrence, this is referred to as "trigger behavior." This kind of behavior is usually preceded and followed by a violent outburst. They are often vocal or nonverbal behaviors that elicit feelings of abandonment and rejection.4. How do you detect a trigger in a child?

To identify triggers in a kid, you need to explain and define the bodily emotions that are connected with triggers. After a tantrum or breakdown, discuss with your kid the sensations they experience in their body. Discuss things like racing heartbeats, heated red cheeks, and lumps in the neck that suggest your child's anger is rising. These methods can help you assess whether your kid has been triggered.

Chapter 7 Consistency, consistency!

Calm Parenting: How to Regain Control When Your Child Annoys You

Why is it so difficult to manage our wrath around our children? There are various causes, but I believe the primary one is that we allow ourselves to become irritated and lose control. When we respond emotionally to our children and lose control, we enable them to choose our conduct rather than the other way around.

Too frequently, parents respond to their children without thinking. Parents assume they must quickly bring their children under control, rather than stopping to ponder, "Wait, let me first get myself under control before I react to my kid."

The greatest strategy to prevent yourself from losing control is to understand what triggers you and to notice when you start to lose control. This is a vital skill for parents to possess. Fortunately, it is a skill that parents can teach their children.

When you attempt to govern your child's behavior instead of your own, you're saying, 'I'm out of control.' I need you to change for me to feel better. Here's a secret: once you get yourself under control, your kids will typically follow suit. Remember that both calm and worry are contagious. It has been established that a parent's fear about their kid adds greatly to their child's uneasiness.

Consider this: if you can't become calm and in charge, you're creating the very environment you're trying to avoid.

Here's an illustration. Assume you're teaching your youngster how to ride a bike. Your child is not comprehending and is irritable, cranky, and talking back to you. Your sentiments are a combination of anger, frustration, rage, and disappointment. You feel responsible to teach him how to ride this bike, but he refuses to cooperate.

Then you holler at your youngster, who is still struggling. Then it grows worse since he can't focus because he's terrified. He feels forced to accomplish something, and he responds by failing.

Instead of snapping and reacting, simply ask yourself, "How can I retain my calm so that I can aid my kid get to where he needs to be?"
Remind yourself that you are not responsible for encouraging him to ride the bike; instead, you are responsible for being calm and offering counsel. You may then evaluate the most efficient strategy for supporting him in learning.
Finally, if we lose control and become upset, we will produce the failure that we are striving to prevent. When parents lose control and become upset in front of their children, we're saying, "There are no grown-ups at home." We're revealing that we can't cope with our anxiousness. And when you attempt to govern your child's behavior instead of your own, you're saying, "I'm out of control." I need you to change for me to feel better."

Nobody wants to lose control and become angry—not it's something we do on purpose. But it simply seems to happen. There are, luckily, things you can do to teach yourself to stay calm. The strategies described below will help you manage your anger and remain cool while dealing with your kid.
Make a Promise To Maintain Control
Commit to working hard to keep control from now on. Take notice of what frustrates you—is it your kid ignoring you? Or does backtalk drive you insane?

It is not always easy to retain control, and no one can manage their anger completely all of the time. Nonetheless, resolve to remain calm and work toward that goal.

The first strategy is generally to simply commit to not saying anything, to not responding at all when the sensation of rage towards your kid emerges. Allow yourself a minute to do whatever you need to do to feel more at ease. I make my way out of the room. I occasionally go into the bedroom or bathroom, but only for a few seconds. Remember, there is no harm in unplugging. You are not compelled to respond to your kid. Be Prepared for Your Child to Push Your Buttons

When our children do not do what we expect of them, we feel frustrated. They either do not listen or do not cooperate.

I suppose the best answer is to anticipate and accept that your kid will press your buttons and not take it personally. In a way, your kid is performing her job—she is pushing her limitations.

Similarly, you must retain your cool and ensure that your kid learns where the limits are and that she is held responsible when she crosses them.

As a parent, realize what you are and are not accountable for.

Some parents are unclear about who they are and what they are accountable for. And when parents take responsibility for things that belong to their children, they become upset.

Keep track of what belongs to you and what belongs to your kid. In other words, what should be in your box, and what should be in your child's box?

A box has limits and personal space within those bounds. Your ideas, emotions, and tasks are all confined within your box. Your child's box includes his ideas, emotions, and responsibilities.

Once you've determined whose box is whose, parents should stay in their box and stay out of their child's box. This does not infer that you do not parent; rather, it suggests that you affect your kid but do not dominate him.

Your kid has tasks in life that he must execute. Those are stored in his box. Those are your child's, not yours.

If you consistently believe you're accountable for how things end out, you'll be in your child's way, which will create extra tension and anxiety.

A parent who successfully stays out of her kid's box might comment to her youngster, "I'm responsible for aiding you in deciding how to address the matter." But I'm not responsible for addressing the situation for you."

If you feel responsible for addressing your child's worries, he will not feel the impulse to remedy them on his own. You'll grow irritated and angrier as you strive harder and harder. And the more you try, the less your kid will try. It's unproductive.
Parents do have duties. When needed, parents should train their children. And parents should set family standards and keep their children answerable to those rules by applying suitable consequences.
The child is liable for the rest.
Related reading: How to Give Effective Consequences to Children
Don't be worried about the future.
Sometimes we look ahead and wonder if this is how our children will be for the rest of their lives. We are worried about how students will perform in the real world if they do not finish their schoolwork.
The more we ponder about their future, the more nervous we grow. We begin to doubt whether we are doing a good job as parents. We are scared that we will not be able to bring them under our control.

Thinking mistakes are a phrase used by psychologists. Thinking mistakes are thoughts we hold in our brains that do not correlate to reality and are often unpleasant and self-defeating. One such cognitive error is our natural inclination to forecast the worst possible result for a given scenario. Things never turn out as horrible as we expected. It appears that our brains prefer scaring us.

As a consequence, remain in your box and concentrate on what you can achieve right now. The future is up to your kid, and no matter how hard you try, you have no control over it. And if you do attempt, your concern will merely escalate, making things worse for both of you.

Prepare Yourself for Anxiety

Take notice of what produces your worry and attempt to prepare for it. Every day at five o'clock, you could feel your family's tensions straining. Everyone has come home from work or school, is hungry, and is decompressing.

"How am I going to manage this when I know my adolescent is going to come raving at me?" What do I do when she begs to use the vehicle even though she knows I'll say no?"

Prepare yourself for the fight you know is coming today.

"This time, I'm not going to dispute with her," you tell yourself. Nobody can force me to do so. I'm not giving her permission to upset me."

"No matter how hard you try to lure me into an argument, it's not going to happen," you should say. Allow yourself to be directed by how you want to regard yourself as a parent rather than your emotional reactions.

Make Use of Positive Self-Talk

Speak to yourself. Yes, communicate with oneself. You may convince yourself in your thinking, "I'm not going to react to my child's actions." I'm going to take a step back. "Let me take a big breath." Self-talk may appear to be a gimmick, but it is a powerful tool. For decades, behavior psychologists have known about the influence of positive self-talk. You may teach your inner voice to encourage serenity rather than anxiety.

"What has benefitted me in the past?" ask yourself. Consider what has previously helped you manage your anxiety. What has helped you deal with something that makes you uncomfortable?

Say something to yourself anytime you sense your emotions increasing. It could vary from "Stop," "Breathe," or "Slow down" "Does it matter?" or "Is this that important?" Experiment with different words and phrases to help you maintain control.

I keep a mental picture handy to help me relax. I remember a magnificent spot that I enjoy and that always relaxes me. Try to imagine that mental image for yourself. Visualizing that destination ahead of time will boost your power to go there more effortlessly when you feel frustrated with your youngster.

Take a Long, Deep Breath

When you discover yourself rising, take a deep breath and stop to think things through. There is a big contrast between responding and reacting. When you respond, you are committing some attention to what you want to convey.

When you reply, on the other hand, you're functioning on autopilot. It's all reactionary.

You want to respond as carefully as possible to what your youngster says or does. Make sure you take a deep breath before replying to your child as the added time will help you to think about what you want to say.

To keep a pot from boiling over, merely remove the top for a few seconds to allow it to air.

Imagine a Happy Relationship with Your Child.

Consider your ideal relationship with your child in five or 10 years. "Is the way I'm acting to my child now going to help me create the relationship I want?" "Will my response aid me to reach my goal?"

This does not suggest that you should give in to your child's wishes or condone his or her poor behavior. Instead, it means that you treat your baby with the same respect that you would want her to regard you. It requires speaking to your baby in the method in which you would like your youngster to talk to you. Maintain a mental picture of the perfect relationship at all times. Make that image your aim. "Will my wrath be worth it?" you should ask yourself. Would your reply move you closer to your purpose of building a stable relationship with your child?

Conclusion

When your kid is troubling you, your thought process is essential. The idea is to be as objective as possible in our own and our child's activities.

"What is my child doing right now?" What is he attempting? Is he responding to the stress in the house?"

You don't have to convince her to listen, but you do need to grasp what's going on and determine how you're going to react to what's occurring. Then you can keep on track and avoid giving in to counter-productive wrath.

The cognitive process itself contributes to our relaxation. What we want to know as parents is, "What can I do to make myself feel better?"

The less we have to say, the better. And the more we think about it, the better the result will be. That is the crux of what we are talking about here: responding deliberately rather than reacting.

"Response derives from the term obligation," someone once stated. In this way, regulating our anger means accepting responsibility for how we want to behave rather than responding automatically when our buttons are touched.
And if we can get our thoughts out ahead of our emotions, we will be better parents. That is the aim.